# Minimalis

Learn Secret Strategies on Living a Minimalist Lifestyle For Your House, Digital Whereabouts, Family Life & Your Own Mindset! Declutter Your Life For Finding Inner Happiness!

By Sofia Madsen

**Table of Contents**

# Introduction

When you were to walk into a room, what is the first thing you would see? A painting? The decor? The leftover sandwich wrapper on the coffee table?

Of all the things you saw, what sticks with you the most? The painting may have been beautiful; it may have even shocked you. The decor may have been relaxing, but it is the wrapper that sticks in your mind. Moreover, why is that exactly? Why do clutter and disorganization remain in our mind's eye long after we have left a room or destination?

Are we secretly neat freaks on the hunt to clear all the trash in the world away? Alternatively, are we programmed to find what does not belong?

I would vote the latter to be safe. From the time we are born, our brains undergo a specific chemical phenomenon called categorization. We seek to organize, collect, and simplify all information that comes in contact with our being. So when a small child cries due to the peas touching the carrots, it's not a huge disaster, just a brief signal to the brain screaming "Error, Error, Error!!!."

As we grow, our brains seek to correct these errors, sometimes we acknowledge them, but more often than not, we completely ignore them, leaving our lives in chaos. We accumulate, collect, and spiral into a continuous mode of "but it's pretty" or "Yes, I need it" when we don't. The clutter and unnecessary items build up over time, and when we look around, we are surrounded by so many things that do not bring us freedom, add value or beauty to our lives.

Life is too short to live with the clutter and too beautiful to be stuck with the extra baggage. Millions have people have come to the same conclusion and have decided to try minimalism.

To understand the facets of why we aim to minimize both our impact on the earth and maximize our impact on each other; each chapter will tackle an essential aspect of our lives and how applying minimalism principles improves your overall quality of life. Gaining insight into the core concept of minimalism is supported by three simple questions: Does it add value to your life? Do you find it beautiful? Does it grant you freedom?

With these three questions, you will gain a better understanding of why we choose to live a minimalistic life and hope you will as well.

# Does It Add Value To Your Life?

"The ultimate value of life depends upon awareness and the power of contemplation rather than upon mere survival."

Aristotle

# Chapter 1: What Is Minimalism?

Minimalism has a long history, but the name itself is fairly new. For the last 8,000 years or more different religions and cultures have practiced the concept of "Letting go to attain spiritual wisdom and understanding." This will be fully discussed in chapter 12, as for now, the name minimalism came about in the 1950s and 60s. It was first used to describe art in the early 1700s and design, later it made its way to define the lifestyle of a small group of people.

Over the last ten years, it has taken off with many considering the catalysis to be the crash of the housing market in 2008. We as a society have made it acceptable to have more than we need with no regard to simply giving away the old when the new is introduced. This is not to say that there aren't kind souls in the world who go above and beyond to make the world a better place, there are, but there are also individuals who choose to reduce their impact on the world by making better overall choices.

Knowing the history of something does not always constitute to you knowing the current trends and the way if affect individual lifestyles. Minimalism is the practice of focusing on the items or people that bring value, beauty, and freedom into our lives and reducing the factors the hold us from attaining a life of essentials. Minimalism is more than just a trend when you consider the deep facets and the teachings grounded in history. If you still need a bit of convincing, think about what we learned of the early nomadic tribes of the world, they only carried around what they needed to survive rather than a whole year worth of food and clothing. They adapted to their environment to make the best of their lives in the wild.

# Myths about Minimalism

It's easy to misunderstand the message that Minimalism hopes to share with the rest of the world. There are so many theories and opinions on how it works and whether or not it is sustainable in the long run. Minimalism, unlike fad diets, has been around since the dawn of time with a constant focus of making people's lives simpler.

Despite its long history, there are still plenty of myths about minimalism and why people decide to take the "path less traveled by".

## The Four Myths of Minimalism

### Myth 1: Minimalist only own a set number of items.

There is and never will be a set number of items a minimalist can own. Each person's approach to the lifestyle differs from the other. While some follow the "One In, One Out" Rule, others may follow the "One In, Two Out" Rule. These rules, like many others regarding the lifestyle, are not set in stone, but they do allow for us to reduce the clutter we are prone to have in our surroundings.

### Myth 2: Minimalism is a nomadic lifestyle

Minimalists are often confused as nomads, this like many other myths and misconceptions about them are false. Some minimalists are nomads, some nomads are not minimalists. Instead, they are travelers exploring the world and the mysteries of the people and places that they visit. Nomads like the freedom that they have to both travel and work at the same time, a lot of minimalists like their steady jobs and abode to come back to each and every day. They are not to be confused.

## Myth 3: Minimalists are vegan/vegetarian

There is nothing wrong being a vegan or vegetarian, but most minimalists eat whatever they want, whenever they want to. They are people just like the rest of us living their lives in a fashion befitting their ideals. It would be rude to condemn an individual based on what they do not eat. Choosing to live an alternate/sustainable lifestyle is about whether you eat meat or not and more about how it benefits you and those around you.

## Myth 4: Minimalists must live in a tiny house

It is a common myth to believe that the majority of minimalists live in tiny houses with a garden and a solar roof. The only correct part of the previous statement is that it is a myth. Many people who do not practice minimalism have taken to the trend of tiny houses and why not, they are creative outlets for the cluttered mind. Tiny houses are the culmination of months of planning followed by a dedication to a smaller lifestyle. Minimalists can have tiny houses but a large majority live in a normal size house with their family and pet.

## Beyond The Myth

Rather than believe everything you hear about Minimalism; it is best to take a moment and understand why the value of space and time has become such an important concept in today's society. It is time to change the narrative of our world and disregard the myths that separate people and believe in the tales that bring us together. That should be the true goal of our minimalism practice.

# Misconceptions about Minimalism

There are plenty of misconceptions, myths, and even some lies about minimalism. None of them are quite true, but they all have a bit of the truth in their origin. Minimalism, like many alternate lifestyles, seeks to have a smaller impact on the world around us. We seek to minimize the time spent on non-essential things and take a look at the bigger picture. We want to emphasize the value of people, things, places, and feelings to get back to a community mindset rather than individualism. We can accomplish so much more when we work together rather than working against each other in our lives.

## The Four Major Misconceptions About Minimalists

Since there are a lot of misconceptions about minimalism, it is best to correct them before we go any further. We want to present the truth behind why we live this lifestyle and how applying it to different areas of your life will help you to live a calmer and simpler life. Yes, you will still have stress and the world may get a bit more chaotic as life goes on but think about what you can accomplish by only getting by with your essentials. This means your essential relationships, connections, books, and household items. Minimalism could change your life in such a powerful way, but only if you let it.

### Misconception 1: Minimalists are not sentimental.

Call me crazy but as a minimalist, a lot of things are either given away or thrown away. That shirt from second grade when you got an "A" on your math test, gone. The hat you got your first kiss in, gone. With so many things that we give away or donate it may come across that we lack sentiment. This is simply not true, minimalists are some of the most sentimental people I know, they just choose to place value in different areas.

We do not get rid of everything from our childhood or that have special memories to us, our goal is to minimize. So instead of your favorite hat that you got your first kiss in, keep it, as long as your significant other does not have a problem with it, you don't have to throw it away. What you should get rid of are the lifejackets that you don't use, the hockey equipment that you haven't used in 20 years, and the baby clothes from your 30-year-old daughter. Give it away so that someone else can find the same joy that you did when you were using them. Clear out the garage and find a new way to spend your time and money. You can save for a vacation with all the new money you can make from selling your old things or pick up a new hobby now that you have space for it.

Giving away the things you no longer need does not make you lack emotion or ruin the memory; you are accepting the importance that the object or person had in your life and choosing to move on to something better. After all, how can you pick up something new when your hands are full, by letting a few things go you are preparing your heart and mind for a new adventure.

## Misconception 2: Minimalists only have ugly clothes.

You may not know it, but there is a fashion trend that uses simple lines and techniques to make bold statements. Minimalist fashion is neither boring nor ugly, designers from all over the world have taken inspiration from the idea of clothes having value. Instead of buying multiple pieces of the same clothes at a low price, buying something at a better quality that will last you several years. That is not to say that you have money to spend on random clothes or accessories, you will still need to spend wisely.

Many minimalists have closets filled with clothes; some just choose to stick to a certain color to simplify the shopping experience. You can choose a  color that goes well with your complexion and buys a few quality pieces that will last you a few years. As your style changes, give away the old clothes as you acquire new ones. Your style can be as creative as you want it to be, just try to minimize the number of clothes that you have. Don't place value in the clothes that you have but in the person that you are and want to become.

## Misconception 3: Minimalists are boring people.

When it comes to minimalism the perception that other people have played an important role in the misconception they might develop. Some people may perceive that minimalists do not go out and have fun because it costs money, they only wear one color clothing because they wish to save money, that they are so focused on minimalizing that they miss out on the "cool stuff."

Minimalists have yet to miss the "cool stuff", rather they are the "cool stuff", they are the adventurers, the writers, the explorers, and the travelers. They find value in different things and seek to understand and help others in the world around them.

Minimalists have sought to find their own adventure, whether at home or aboard.

## Misconception 4: Minimalists are extreme environmentalists.

Being an environmentalist has never been a bad thing in my book. They truly care about the earth and wish to educate the masses. Some minimalists are environmentalists, but it is not a general rule that you have to be an environmentalist. Minimalist by nature use fewer resources and disregard less waste, this, in turn, is better for the environment. And this is what we generally want, to be better for the environment and to use fewer resources in our journey to a better world for future generations. Minimalists can be whatsoever they desire to be, that is, including an environmentalist.

## Disregarding the Myths and Misconceptions

Minimalism is truly an art form, taking the things we find essential to our existence and treasuring them regardless of what others may think or believe. We also do not mind discarding the things that no longer bring value to our lives. While there are plenty of misconceptions, even myths are meant to be proven whether true or false. We hope that each chapter will open a new door for you and bring ideas and concepts for you to think about. Taking a step into a new world can be quite frightening, minimalism welcomes you with two arms because using only one would not bring value to your life or beauty to ours. We hope you find freedom from the clutter and create a mind of gratitude.

# Chapter 2: Relationships

When you think about minimalism and relationships, it is really hard to not to make a satirical joke about having one friend that ticks all the boxes. One friend for working out with, one who cooks good food, one friend that you work with, one friend who is funny (I honestly hope you have more than one friend who is funny) and one friend to make up for what the others lack.

That should be it, right?

Wrong. Friends should not be only categorized with what the person can add to your life and how they can benefit you. That is called a parasitic relationship, rather than one built on mutual trust and respect.

Relationships should be treated in the same way. You should aim to build valuable relationships with other people in the hope of growing your view of the world. These relationships can always vary in value, but what you hope to accomplish is the positive relationships that expand over time, regardless of whether you are in constant contact with the person or not.

# Minimalism and Relationships

A minimalist relationship is raw in its origin. It is based on mutual trust and respect, with the foundation never straying too far from creating a meaningful existence. If minimalism is the act of clearing the clutter in order to find the essentials of life, then a minimalistic relationship is the act of clearing the unnecessary relationships in order to find meaningful and long-lasting friendships.

You may ask why it is important to clear the clutter out of your life in terms of relationships; in order for you to find truly breathtaking relationships, you must first know what it is that you're looking for. You must ask yourself what it is that you value, how can these relationships help you to be a better individual, will the next friendship you make be the one that helps you overcome a certain fear or go on an adventure? If you take a few moments out of your daily life to consider these questions you will see whether or not your relationships are minimalistic or simply superficial.

if you realize that you have a superficial relationship you may not be the only one, not all relationships that minimalist is truly minimalistic. As we are not perfect people and we do not always see the inner workings of a person's mind when we first meet them. take the last friendship that you make and analyze it, what was the basis of your friendship was built on? did you have a similar hobby that you liked? was this a work friend? are you connected through mutual acquaintances?

Seems like a lot of questions for just a small friend doesn't; at the end of the day, your friendships are important. Some people go as far as to say that the friends you make are sometimes better than the family you have. Whether this statement is true will definitely depend upon your family and what your friends are like. In this chapter, we will address how relationships affect the way you network and by thinning out those relationships you can be a better worker, a better friend, and a better family member. The goal is to make sure that you see the value in your friendships and relationships by first identifying what it is that you value and how it helps to make you a better person at the end of the day.

## Minimizing Your Inner Circle

Let's first talk about your inner circle and how you can minimize it to make it more effective and efficient. What were young and we decide to have friends that are close enough for us to share the secrets our parents tell us to never tell anyone about, they are the beginning of our inner circle. When we're older and we decide to have secrets and tell our inner circle, sometimes it does not go as well as we hoped. What makes one's inner circle better than another and how can we as minimalist or future minimalist create inner circles that are worthy of our goals in life to minimalize the things that take away from our essentials.

How do you evaluate your inner circle? How do you know that your inner circle will help you to reach your goals rather than hold you back? You make love with a simple answer and say that you're in a circle has people who will help you reach your goals and forward your career to the path that you wanted to go to. and while that makes sense it's not always true. let's talk about evaluating Your Inner Circle and how you can minimize it while maximizing the potential of a lifelong friendship and like-minded individuals.

## How to evaluate your inner circle

In order to minimize your inner circle, you must first create a definition of what your inner circle should look like. Our inner circle is made up of people who we want to be like or who find inspirational in achieving our goals and dreams. By Nature humans are tribal but that is never to be viewed as a bad thing. Our individualistic selves should be celebrated especially when it comes to creating an inner circle.

Take, for example, a freshman college student just starting out on their new adventure, trying to decide their major, juggling working and studying at the same time, and to top that all off they have to find friends who helped him through their college years and hopefully beyond. They were told college is going to be the best four years of their lives and now they're looking at 5 years with a major that they're not even sure will help them make a living. This is where a good support group can come in handy and help you actually carry through on your plans and dreams in order to make your life better.

Now, if you are college treated most of us already knows you don't necessarily know yourself as much as you could. you spent a lot of time trying to decide who you are and what you stand for. And the sad truth is this does not change when you reach the adult world and start a career. To this day, we are still trying to figure out who we are and where we go from here. Hopefully, the answer is nowhere but up. Your college years go by you will realize that you are more than just a number you are unique. You have your own ideas about who you would like to be and where you'd like to go. By starting early to evaluate what your Friendship Circle and your inner circle should look like you will be able to minimize the negativity and stress that often follows with forming meaningful relationships.

### Define Yourself

Your thoughts decide your action and your actions decide your character. before you are able to evaluate your relationships around you-you need to be able to evaluate yourself. find who you are and how you would like to move forward in life. by outlining these small details you'll better understand how to relate to other people.

Define who you are: are you an introvert or an extrovert, do you prefer to cook at home or would you like to go out to eat, are you ambitious or lazy. these are the things that you should take into consideration before you start to look for other people to spend time with. if you want to take on the world you must first know yourself and by knowing yourself you'll be able to better understand why people do the things they do. Before you can minimize you must first understand what is present, then you would be able to separate the essential from the superficial.

## Define Your Goals

When we are young we have all these dreams and goals that would like to achieve. By the time you graduate college, we've been beaten down so much that we forget why we started college in the first place. We forget why we wanted to learn and to grow and to discover. in order to evaluate those around you must first remember your goals in your dreams. One who does not remember their goals and dreams is simply walking around without a map of where they would like to go and the destinations they would like to explore.

This is not to say that if you have never been to college that you cannot have goals; a false statement. Your goals are not determined by the degree in your hand but by how hard you work and what you are willing to sacrifice to attain them. Some of the most influential people in the world have never stepped foot in a college well that is, except to make, you know, a speech. Take a moment to jot down a few goals that you would like to achieve in your lifetime. You can create a 10, a 20, or a 30-year plan. As long as you seek to improve yourself and seek information in order to make your minimalist journey to the top there's no one that could stop you except yourself. When defining your goals, you are laying out your foundation of where you want to go. We'll dig deeper into defining goals in chapter 4 but for now, I want you to go ahead and define who you want to be in life, where you would like to go and see how much of a difference it makes it who you choose to surround yourself with.

## Define Your Morals

What you stand for is an important aspect of Who You Are. If you are an environmentalist, then will stand up for the environment. If you are a herbalist you will stand up for the importance of using herbs in our daily lives.

If you decide to become a minimalist you will stand up for the things that you find essential and disregard those that clutter your life. Good morals are similar, if you have bad morals or if you do not stand for anything you will simply agree with everything. there will be no difference between you and the person next to you as you will have lost your uniqueness. what deciding what friendships and relationships hold having a moral compass can help you decide who to surround yourself with which is very similar to having goals.

If your moral compass points you into the direction of saving the planet then you will decide that anyone or anything that does not value the planet is not a part of your inner circle. On the other hand, if your moral compass points you in the direction that harms the planet, you will be pointed into the direction where waste is something you truly cherish. There's a stark difference between having a good moral compass and a bad.

Choose your moral compass and choose your inner circle. Wisely

## Asking The Right Questions: The Friendship ROI Model

When it comes to making friends it can be quite difficult in the adult world, but that's not mean it should stop you from getting the most benefit out of the friendships that you make. In order for you to maximize your friendship let's consider the Friendship ROI Model. The Friendship ROI Model takes its foundation from the ROI Model, The Return On Investment Model. This model's focus is to gain interest in what was originally invested in stocks. If you apply it to relationships, you can smoothly create lasting friendships that grow over time.

In order to start a Friendship ROI Model, be sure to ask yourself the three questions of minimalism.

### Question #1: Does it add value to your life?
Value is subjective to the individual.

### Question #2: Do you find it beautiful?
Beauty is subjective to the viewer.

### Question #3: Does it grant you freedom?
Freedom is subjective to the survivor.

After you've answered these three questions go ahead and invest in the friendship and see the beauty that it blooms in your life. In 50, years you'll be thankful for the friendships that you've made and your investment in order to pursue your personal and career goals

## Efficient Work Relationships

Finding work and life balance can be hard and for some people, it's nearly impossible, but with minimalism, you be able to eliminate a lot of the stressors from work and be able to enjoy your time at home. This may sound like a far-fetched idea, however, if you think about minimalizing the work and stress that you have in your day today you can maximize the time you have to relax. Minimalizing is about thinking simple and providing solutions that work for people in their everyday lives. This is not to say that every solution provided will be for you but you can take each solution and see how they are applicable in your life.

In order for you to easier navigate the office politics, find a job that you love. Yes, this can take some time as you may think that your dream job it's not the job for you after a few years of working in a specific field. Find supportive co-workers, they can help make the struggle of office politics so much easier to deal with. Before you start your job, discuss your role and salary. Create boundaries in order for you to not be taken advantage of in the workplace.

You should also try to find like-minded co-workers that can help you with your work and help you through the different tasks you may receive upon first starting a job. Find a job that you think it's valuable that makes your life and those around you happier. Take a moment to try and find simple solutions too complicated questions and remember to congratulate yourself if no one else does. By using you simple tactics you will be able to find yourself in better working conditions and mental space.

One of the best tips we could ever give you about minimalizing the stress at work is remembering to take a vacation. You can't solve all the problems of your workplace and you shouldn't try to unless that's your job. What you can do is make your workplace better by doing your best. Take a few moments to read back over the last few paragraphs and jot down any extra ideas you may have is how you can minimalize the amount of stress you have from work.

Remember to treat yourself. Yes, I said it treat yourself. You are part of a collective whole and that collective whole, unfortunately, can go on without you. Ensure that you don't burn out or break down along this journey and if you need to take a break, do so.

## Family Matters

Families make up a huge part of our ecosystem and for some individuals, families can be extremely complicated. When considering minimalizing familial relationships, think of ways to get the best out of each interaction that you have with your family. Minimize the stress and maximize the overall enjoyment of being a unit.

Create an environment in which love and understanding can come forth, which in the end will save your sanity. If it's for your own family, as an adult, you should teach quality over quantity, finding beauty in their surroundings rather than looking for superficial fluff. If you are a child of a family, aim to be understanding. Minimalize misunderstandings by looking from a different point of view at a problem.

But at the end of the day, if you're from a dysfunctional family, it is okay to eliminate toxic people from your life. Never sacrifice your sanity for those who rather see you in a less fortunate situation: that is included but not limited to your family. Avoid negative emotions and situations by striving to find the best in each situation. No, it's not necessary to be over-optimistic, but when going forward it is possible to help to navigate strenuous familial relationships.

Find the value in each one of your familiar relationships and minimize the stress of each interaction. Ask yourselves the three questions: does this relationship add value to my life, are there beautiful moments in this relationship, does this relationship grant me freedom and allow to be my best self? If the answer is no to all three questions and feels free to cut these people out of your lives. This does not mean that you lack sentiment or that you are ungrateful, it simply means that you value for relationships that build you up rather than tear you down. Learn to be okay with saying no even if it's your family.

# The Value Of Relationships

Each encounter that you have has the possibility of being a lifelong friendship/ relationship.   finding out the difference between which relationships you keep and which relationships you let go can be half the struggle and a lot less fun.  By implementing different minimalistic ideas you can find the best relationships for your life and your career. place value in your relationships and evaluate them on the ROI model.   By investing in your relationships you'll be able to guarantee a better outcome and learn which ones to keep and which ones to throw away. Take care of your relationships and they will take care of you.

# Chapter 3: Time Management

I want to tell you a secret, now, you have to make sure that you keep it between us and you can't tell anybody else that does not read this book.

Are you ready?

Minimalists are not as productive as you may think. What they are is extremely organized. Well, maybe not extremely organized, but they are organized, it's what we pride ourselves on. When contemplating whether or not, we should take on a new project: we check our schedules. We take a look to see what we have going on and what's coming up in the next few weeks. This way we can see whether or not we're able to add a new project or list of things to do or if we should wait for a more appropriate time.

Are you confused about why this is a secret? Don't be! My secret is actually a well-known fact among minimalists, but I'm happy to let you in on it.

You see, your productivity it's tied to how well you organize yourself and manage your time. This chapter will talk about how to get the best out of your date, how to organize the faces of your work week, what you're doing wrong with productivity, why multitasking is just not working out for you, and why you should learn to plan ahead.

## Hacking Your Productivity

Time management isn't solely about the time it's also about how you plan each moment for efficient productivity. When you prioritize the important tasks you'll be able to hack your productivity for a better day and work week. Change your point of view on productivity, think of time management as a way of organizing your life to gain peace.

To be productive you must first list your goals for the day, there's a higher chance of actually completing these goals after writing them down and having them visible in front of you. You begin to work you realize that you have less time to care about what is going on in front of you take a break. It is an important part of minimalism to rest. You may notice from time to time that you have the diminishing motivation, in these moments simplify your life by setting three times that you have to do each day. make the remaining top optional, this way you're able to complete your initial goal and get extra work done.

When confronted with a difficult task, find what makes the task valuable to you. If you're able to create worth in relation to the task at hand then it will seem easier to accomplish. Minimalist often prayer ties in such a way that toss can be completed in a day or two. If it is a longer project, then a task may need several other days or months to be completed however there is always a plan and how to get it done.

If you're able to change how you think about time management I'm getting projects done, then you would be able to be more productive in your daily life. Minimalism does not require you to have a hundred sticky notes in five different directions, it requires you to think carefully about what is important to you and what you can gain from it. Hacking your productivity is just one small step to minimalize in your entire life.

## You're (Probably) Multitasking Wrong?

Do you know how to multitask? Or let's ask a better question do you know how to confuse your brain in five different directions?

Given how confusing the idea of multitasking can be your answer my probably be to the second question rather than the first. Multitasking is doing multiple things at once and hopefully doing it correctly. You may have been told in school that learning how to multitask is an important part of time management. And in some aspects, it really is an important part of time management but that does not mean it's always correct to do it. It is wise to learn when and where multitasking will be most efficient for your day.

Take the minimalistic approach to multitasking where should you start? Should you start at the easiest test that's there and one of the hardest tasks and do them at the same time? Should you do simple tasks at the same time thus giving you the most efficient route to completing all the tasks you have for today?

Never multitask with large projects at hand, this will cause great confusion and often lead to mistakes that are better left not being made. You can multitask with small tasks such as cooking. If you are cooking a small meal multitasking is a great idea in order to get it done on time. If you're cooking a large meal focus only on one part of the meal at a time that way you're short not to make mistakes and ruin the dish.

Multitasking is not for everyone and that's something we need to be able to tell others. You don't have to multitask. If it's not a skill that you have or something that you're able to do well, then don't do it.

Repeat after me: I don't know how to multitask and that's okay, I will just do one task at a time and do it well.

Let this be your mantra for multitasking, if it's not a skill that you possess, don't worry about it just do the best that you can.

## Planning Ahead

There's a surprisingly simple quote that says "if you fail to plan, then you plan to fail". An important part of minimalism is planning, such as when you decide to Buy a new piece of furniture if you follow the one in one out rule then you'll be getting rid of another piece of furniture to make space for the new one. with careful planning, you will be able to make the most of each and every purchase that you make. but planning ahead is not limited to just purchases think about it as if you went on a vacation or if you had goals. by taking a few moments the plan ahead you are effectively making your day goes smoother and your trip more enjoyable.

### Choose Your Moments

When we think about planning ahead we often think about writing things down and making sure everything is mapped out perfectly. I want you to change that way of thinking rather than making sure everything is mapped out perfectly why don't we choose our moments. What does take moments to be intentional about what we want and where we want to go.

This is what we mean when we say choose our moments taking time to go and declare what is valuable to us rather than being involved in every single situation that comes our way. We choose how to react and went to react to something that happens. Choosing moments of whether we would like to have somebody inside of our family or have them leave the family.

Being intentional about your choices will make your minimalism journey so much simpler than it could be. Choosing your moments enables you to Define your morals, Define yourself, Define your goals.

## Your Time Is Valuable

Your time like the rest of your life is valuable, refused wasted on meaningless things. take a few moments and write down your goals for today and your daily planner. when you're able to see what you hope to accomplish this makes managing your time so much easier. be intentional about your time and choose the moments that you want to cherish rather than the moments you wish to forget.

# Chapter 4: Goals and Gains

We all have goals and dreams in life that we wish to pursue, choosing a minimalistic lifestyle can help you achieve those goals and have tremendous gains in your personal life. In the last chapter, we talked about time management and how to hack your productivity, in this chapter we want to talk about using those methods in order to achieve your goals. Specifically, we want to talk about choosing the moments and planning ahead. By implementing these methods you are able to create a minimalist lifestyle where you will not have to worry about how you're going to achieve the goals you just have to work towards them.

That may sound a bit far-fetched to you but think about the big picture here.

Refuse to think small when you're thinking about minimalism and how to achieve your goals. A rather ironic statement trust me I know but minimalism is by no means a small or minute way of life. Minimalism considers the larger things that hand and then act upon it in order to value what is most important and most essential rather than things that take our time away from them. So choose your moments in this next chapter and think about your goals where you want to be. Think about the goals that you had when you were a child and how far you have strayed from them.

There's nothing more painful than realizing that you have disappointed your childhood self. Minimalism can give that back to you. It can help you to realize what goals you had as a child and how to incorporate those into your daily life. The tools you gain with minimalism is far greater than the things you lose. Yes, you will have to give away a few things and yes you will have to say no to a few thin but your life will be filled with so much value, joy, beauty, and freedom that you won't need all the things that you've given up.

## The Reward of Working Hard

Many people are obsessed with rewards. They crave prizes and recognition for their hard work. Hundreds of occasions you likely heard this sentence, "You have to work intelligently, not hard." To make the correct decisions is to be clever. Intelligent people move really quickly up the ladder. But the significance of hard labor is valued. Before you reaped the benefits of achievement, your idols, heroes, and every successful person you know have worked hard and made significant contributions.

When they achieved their goals, they became more experienced, committed fewer errors, enhanced their decision-making abilities and chosen career paths. This saved them a lot of energy, time, and effort. You can only shoot your best and work hard for your objectives. You must never forget how precious it is to work hard. Minimalism teaches the importance of hard work and the benefit of simple solutions and outcomes.

Don't wait for opportunities to come your way, go generate possibilities of success for your future. You have the capacity to work hard rather than run from hard work, regardless of what is needed to accomplish your large objectives.

You may stumble across barriers that prevent others who are less determined. But what does that bringing you? Where does hard work take you? A genuinely successful individual will continue to struggle until their craft is perfected. The achievement of your goals depends on the level of hard work that you put in.

If minimalism is about changing your mindset so that you may change your life, then hard work has to be one of its pillars for success. You will not be able to reach great heights without the blood, sweat, and tears of working hard. Take this chapter to heart as it can change your life in a spectacular way.

## Visualizing: The Big Picture

There is no such thing as the perfect minimalist, minimalism is built on imperfection, hard work, and dedication. We seek to be understanding of our surroundings by focusing on what is important rather than what is simply there. Oftentimes we miss the universe while focusing on the Stars. let us take time to look at the big picture in this section and see how minimalism can help us to appreciate what is greater than ourselves.

Before we start talking about the big picture is important to know that perfection is simply subjective to the intent of an individual. On the same mindset, the intent of an individual is subject to change. We may seek to control our intent but each situation will change what our intentions are. In a minimalistic lifestyle, it is important to make your intentions plain, so that if they do change you will be able to analyze them and evaluate them to see how they impact the bigger picture.

Take a moment here to think about what you truly desire, is it perfect? Or is it simplicity? Our desires guide our intent. And while you might not like the sound of that it is quite true. We are humans based upon our desires and we often act on those sometimes even without thinking. When visualizing the big picture our intent plays an important role in that aspect.

If your desire of a bigger picture it's the focus on how you can help others to achieve their best. Your focus on yourself will decrease, but that does not mean you will no longer care for yourself as a person. You will become a part of the big picture and by doing so you are fulfilling feeling your minimalistic desires. Take pride in your intention to live a minimalistic life, but do not stop at the intention.

Previously, we talked about hard work. It is now time to take your intention and transform it into hard work. Seek for all your days to be better than your yesterdays and your tomorrows to be the greatest intention that you could possibly accomplish.

## Ignore the Masses, Focus on the Few

There are so many Trends in today's society so many fad diets and things that we're all supposed to be doing saying thinking and believing. But does it make sense to always go along with what everybody else is doing? Sure if everybody else is running for their lives you probably should too, but that does not mean that the danger that they're running from is real. You're probably thinking something along the lines of what's going on here? How do I stand for something that I know nothing about to answer that question, honestly, you don't?

Previously, we talked about morals and how you have to define them in order to know where you're going in life. Now we will talk about breaking down those morals in order to have a better understanding of how minimalism can help you navigate through life. What are the core principles of minimalism? And how can they help you to see the big picture?

The big picture is made up of small moments where you strive for the best outcome. Take a moment to think about where you want to go in your life and how ignoring the fads can get you there with a sound heart and mind. With the world changing so fast and people leading lives that are less intrinsic than ever before, it is now up to individuals to reach beyond themselves and live a life of value. The small impacts that we have on our inner circles in the grand scheme of things affect those around us in such a way that years down the line our actions still have consequences.

Minimalize your life in such a way that you decrease the stress around you and increase the peace found on the inside. Many people often think that a minimal life is stressful because you have to count your belongs and always worry about the impact that you have on the world around you. But you may have learned from the first chapter that those are not at the core of minimalism. We focus on the essential things in life to get the greatest benefits. Remember that building long-lasting relationships, just like the other things that you chose to invest in, take dedication and patience.

## Be Absent

An important part of minimalism is learning to be absent. This does not mean that you get out of work or out of school. It actually means taking time out to be present in the things that are more important by being absent in the things that are less important. Being absent is important because then you are putting your energies towards the things that can make you a better person and a better individual. So take a few moments to think of ways you can be absent, maybe this means no longer going to that bar that you normally do and spending more time at home cleaning or clearing out the things that you have neglected.

Being absent takes a lot of practice to get to a place where it does not bother you to miss out on certain things. There are a few ways you could practice absence: if you have a certain hobby that you love to take a few hours every day to learn more about it. Your hobby will allow you to make friendships and add value to your life. With focusing on this small aspect you will move one step closer towards the bigger picture.

## What Brings You Joy
### What makes you happy?

Is it waking up on a rainy day and realizing you get to stay in today? There are a few simple joys that we all have. Minimalism says to focus on those small joys and discover if it brings you joy. There is value in finding the small joys of life. Think back to your favorite memory, think of how that memory has impacted your life and what you believe to be joyful. Remember this feeling and let it guide you to what minimalism could mean to you. A new sense of joy and wellbeing.

### What makes you giggle or laugh out loud?

You may laugh often, or not at all. Whether you like to laugh or not that is up to you. Some individuals only laugh in extremely funny or ironic situations. Dig deep within and find what makes you laugh. The joys of how a smile or laugh can change your life have entire studies in positive psychology. Minimalism provides a certain joy to its practitioners allowing them to enjoy life in a new way.

They are not held down by the stressors of life, rather they are freed from them. Minimalism is more than just a lifestyle change; it also changes your way of thinking. The things that surround you will no longer be what control you. You will have the power to decide whether or not you want to indulge in the simple pleasures of life.

### Essentially, what brings you joy?

This is one of the few parts in the book I wish for you to stop reading a really consider the answers to these questions. Think deeply and aim to unlock some of those ideas or dreams you had when you were younger about what really makes you happy and laugh. If you haven't laughed until you've cried in years, then that's fine as well.

Our goal here is to use minimalism as a catalyst to make you happy and unlock the things that make you want to live a better life. So take a few moments to minimalize the things in your life, especially those that bring you sadness, stress, anger, and frustration. The things that take your attention away from a simpler life, minimize them and move towards a life that celebrates finding joy in moments rather than things and people. Look towards a life of hope, joy, and love. This is not to say that minimalism will make you the happiest person in the world, let's be realistic here. It will open your eyes to see the forest for all its glory, rather than a few meager trees.

## What Are You Grateful For

### Consider what makes you grateful

Gratitude journals have been used by patients of therapists, students of healers, and simply individuals looking to make a positive change within themselves. A gratitude journal is simply a journal where, every day, you write down a few things you are grateful for. At first, these things may be vague and generalized, but as you continue your journal you will be able to recognize events that happen to you throughout your daily experiences that deserve to be recognized and written down.

These journals have been proven to help therapy patients overcome their depression a little bit easier. Even if you don't suffer from a mental illness, you could probably use some of the benefits of a gratitude journal. Some of the benefits listed earlier in this book were:

1. Improved relationships
2. Less stress
3. Better sleep
4. Self-awareness
5. A safe space for thoughts to live

There are many other benefits of a gratitude journal as well, though! It can also help you develop your personality and the way you experience emotions, something many people could certainly improve on. Emotional maturity is a trait that is attractive to potential partners, employers, and new friends. Looking deeper into what you're truly thankful for will help you come to terms with your emotions, teach you where your greed lies, and show you the valuable skill of humility.

Like many other journal formats, a gratitude journal can also teach you to love and respect yourself. Improving your self-esteem is easy to do when you have a concrete, readable list of things you've loved about your own life. When you get down, looking at your previous entries can show you how blessed you really are. (However, as with anything, if the negative feelings become overwhelming, please reach out to a friend or therapist!)

Yet another positive factor of a gratitude journal is that it brings change. If you feel as though you're stagnating in negative feelings and bad experiences, writing down what you're thankful for every day can show you a higher perspective. Once you get into the habit of acknowledging your blessings when you write them in your journal, it will become second nature for you to see the world as a nicer place than before.

When you've started your gratitude journal, you may find other amazing benefits on your own! Be sure to write them down.

Here's an example of an entry in a gratitude journal, selected for continuity:

17 April –
Today I am grateful for...
- Coffee with friends
- My family
- My partner
- A roof over my head
- Freedom of transportation
- Hobbies, like stamp collecting

Even if some of the things you're grateful for today don't remain in your life tomorrow, it's important to remember that nothing is permanent, including tragedy. Writing down all the good things that happen to you or exist in your life right now will give you something to look back at with hope. Things get better.

WHAT YOU'LL NEED

Many people skip the entire process of writing things down on paper and head straight for the digital world. While this may not have some of the same benefits as a physical notebook, it can be very convenient for some individuals. They may be busy professionals who have easier access to a phone than they have to a notebook (or a series of notebooks, if you're really enthusiastic), people with a tendency to lose things, or severely broke college students.

Whatever your background, if you feel as though a pen and paper might cramp your style, absolutely feel free to use the resources available to you! We live in modern times, where content is king and apps run our lives. If you're so connected to your virtual existence that you can't see yourself using something as old and romantic as a paper journal, go ahead and start out by using an app.

Here are some things to consider, however, should you choose to go that route:

1.    Apps can become obsolete.
2.    Data can become corrupt.
3.    Information stored on the cloud can be leaked.
4.    You can't pass a file on to your grandchildren as easily as you could a book.
5.    There is something inherently cathartic about writing with a pen and paper.

All that being said, if you want to experiment with journaling apps, it might be a great way to get you started. As you become more comfortable with the activity of journaling in general, you may be compelled to switch mediums. If not, that's okay too! Not everyone works the same way because our brains are all wired differently from each other.

Here are some of the benefits of journaling on a phone or computer:

1.    There are many programs and apps on the market that can make beginning your journal easier.
2.    It will be easier to transfer text to a file, should you write something so profound you feel the need to share it.
3.    You don't have to worry about carrying anything with you other than your phone, tablet, or laptop, which you would already have had on your person.
4.    It's minimalistic and inexpensive because you already have all the materials you might need.

5.    You will have easy access to forums of people online doing the same thing as you, so you can find inspiration to help get your flow going.

No matter how you choose to begin your journal, this is a purely personal decision and nobody can judge you for it. Your journal is a safe, sacred space for your thoughts and your eyes only. Make it cohesive to your lifestyle. Forcing yourself to do form a habit you're not really comfortable doing will likely result in a very short-lived experience with a new habit. Digital or handwritten, a journal is a journal. It can always migrate to another medium later on if necessary.

MAKING TIME

One option that works well for people who use their journals to keep shorthand notes of important details (rather than writing whole paragraphs) is to keep the journal handy throughout the day and write down what seems important. That way, the focus is shifted from journaling simply for the sake of journaling, to journaling with the goal of keeping notes. This method is usually best accomplished with a small notebook specifically designed to be carried in a pocket or a purse. You can use this method by itself, or you can use it in tandem with a standard journal. This is a great way to make sure busy people can stick with the habit.

If you're wordier, you may prefer to set aside time at the end of every day to write. In this block of time, you can write out how the day went, what happened, and how it made you feel. You can also look forward to the next day, setting goals and making plans.

MAKING IT INTO A HABIT

Making time can be one of the most difficult parts of journaling. A great way to make it easier is to look forward to the experience every day. What do you already do every day that you can associate the developing habit with? Do you sit and enjoy your coffee every morning as part of your daily ritual? Try associating that time with a short journal entry, to begin with. As you keep the habit up, you'll likely feel more compelled to write longer entries with more detail. Eventually, this will be part of your daily life, and all you had to do was bring a notebook to the kitchen table when the coffee was done brewing.

Perhaps you think more clearly at night. What's a nighttime ritual you're already used to? Do you wind down with your dog and a glass of wine? Do you read a book in bed? Try the method suggested earlier; simply bring your notebook along with you. As long as you associate journal time with something you already enjoy, and as long as you keep your first entries simple and stress-free, it will be very easy to make time for your journal. You'll associate it with a relaxing activity, so you'll begin to look forward to it.

You may feel as though you're Pavloving yourself. Keep in mind that the way any good habit is formed is by positive reinforcement. Associating a new task with something you already benefit from will teach you that both activities are rewarding. (In case you're wondering, this goes for any good habit you're trying to begin. Feel free to use this nugget of wisdom next time you have to make yourself do something you're not totally sure you'll enjoy.)

The official average amount of time it takes to form a habit is 66 days. That means if you keep up with your new journal for a little over two months, you'll have developed a habit that, if maintained, could last you for years to come.

The first step to developing a habit, according to some experts, is to associate the new behavior you want with a habit you already have. Our entire lives are comprised of multiple habits of differing variables, one after another.

So let's recap. Go ahead: pick a thing you regularly do at the same time, such as brushing your teeth at night or feeding the dog dinner and begin associating your journal time with that event. (If you plan on using your journal to set daily goals in the morning, try associating journaling with a morning event like making your bed or eating breakfast.)

If you miss a couple of days during your first two weeks, don't sweat it. Keep going the next day, and try to find another regular behavior you already engage in to remind you when it's time to write.

GETTING THINGS OUT OF YOUR HEAD, AND ON PAPER INSTEAD

START WITH GRATITUDE

*Be grateful:* Gratitude journals are extremely helpful to those of us who may struggle to stay positive. When we start or end our day by writing down three or more things we're thankful for, it greatly improves our general outlook on life.

Sometimes life can be so overwhelming that it becomes difficult to pinpoint exactly what good things are happening to us. Even though we know deep down that a lot of our struggles contain some nuggets of positivity, it can be particularly laborious to specify what those silver linings may be.

One of the most frustrating examples of this is when something that's essentially a good thing causes too much stress. Maybe you inherited a windfall, but the resulting legal maze is exhausting and you're beginning to wish you had never received anything at all¬... more money, more problems, after all. Or perhaps you recently welcomed a newborn into the world, and while the child is a blessing, the bills and lack of sleep aren't. Do the stressful parts of these things outweigh the good parts? Absolutely not! However, it's very easy to fall into a cycle of depression by getting overwhelmed by the cons of an otherwise positive, albeit multifaceted, situation. Combat these feelings with a gratitude journal.

SOME BENEFITS OF A GRATITUDE JOURNAL:

BETTER SLEEP. Have you ever tried to sleep the night before an important event, only to find yourself tossing and turning and imagining the worst? A loose grasp on the positive can manifest as fear, and it's almost impossible to fall asleep when you're afraid. The next time you start feeling anxious before bed, writing down what you're thankful for may help you calm your restless mind. If the fear has no apparent root, reading your previous entries in the gratitude journal you keep will help remind you that everything is okay. Going to bed happy and grateful, rather than anxious and lost, will result in sounder sleep, as your heart rate and blood pressure will naturally lower.

SELF-AWARENESS. You can learn a lot about a person by knowing what they cherish the most. We all tend to think we know ourselves better than anyone else ever could, but sometimes this is inaccurate. We may be basing our values on outdated information about ourselves. So how do you learn where your priorities really lie? You guessed it: journaling. Try keeping a gratitude journal for a month; look back later and check out what themes show up the most. If your recurring themes come as a shock to you, use this as a platform for self-discovery and growth.

A SAFE SPACE FOR THOUGHTS TO LIVE. Are you grateful for something you're afraid others will find strange? While those feelings are probably rooted in anxiety, they are still valid and deserve to be written down! Your gratitude journal is, ideally, for your eyes only, so you can put as much weird stuff in there as you want without fear of judgment. This helps you understand yourself, your interests, and your values.

There are so many reasons to be grateful for your gratitude journal!

THE POWER OF WORDS AND SPEAKING THINGS INTO REALITY

There are a lot of old sayings about the power of willing things into existence:

"Ask and ye shall receive."

"Be careful what you wish for."

And of course, my personal favorite from the Book of Proverbs:

"Death and life are in the power of the tongue."

To some people, these sayings seem silly. After all, words are just randomly arranged pieces of the alphabet assigned to concepts. How can you just ask and then, somehow, magically, receive?

The Law of Attraction is a funny thing. It can mean the difference between success and failure. Many people who have reached lofty career goals thank this concept for their achievements. Obviously, the individual is responsible for their own actions and words, but focusing those on one specific goal has been shown, through many success stories, to be effective in cultivating a future beneficial to the individual in question.

This notion that one can simply believe things into being is ancient and withstanding. Part of the reason it works is the inherent power behind words.

# Chapter 5: Technology

What is the purpose of Technology?

And why must we be a slave to it?

If you walk down the street I look left and right there's a high probability that you will run into someone looking at their phone. They may actually be looking for something important, or maybe they're just watching a video, they could even be trying to navigate their way from one place to the next. But that's not the point here, technology has become such a huge part of our daily lives that we forget how to live without it.

However, we shouldn't have to live without technology but we should realize that there are a time and place for everything and often time we use technology to build walls around us as of ways not to interact with the people in our vicinity.

## The Purpose of Technology

The technology was born on the day that man was made or on the day that man appeared on earth for lack of a better explanation. Over the decades, technology has developed from a slow to a quickly moving pace. Of course, to be better for himself a person was born. With technology, he had to do that. Consequently, technology is a component of our conduct. You can call it an epigenetic behavior, and not far from correct. But technology is not randomness. The implementation of science should be technology. This is not randomness. However, it can be categorized as a device for evolution.

Technology takes you from what is probably to what is possible. If we fail to see the gift that technology has given us, then we are no better than children in need of guidance. Minimalism teaches that to focus on the essentials, we must understand why a tool or service is important to us.

Why is technology important to you? Does it help you to do your job? Is it there to help you connect to those that you hold in high regard?

Technology is a tool with no true master and this is something we need to take into consideration. If technology has no master, then has it become our master. The purpose of technology is to explore what is unknown and we often take that for granted. In order not to fall victim to technology we have to be able to recognize when too much retweet and likes will not add value to our lives. Contrary to popular belief,  it actually takes away from the value of our lives if not used correctly.

# The Three Rules To Minimize The Use Of Technology

## Only Buy What You Need

Each year some new technology comes out a new phone, a new headset, or a new laptop. Technologies always updating, evolving, and unfortunately cluttering our houses. When it comes to buying technology is important to only buy what you need instead of what you want. When you buy only what you need you will spend less money and be able to find beauty in the things around you more than on your screen.

This statement also goes out to photographers, it is so easy to buy the latest camera or the latest lens but it will not help you to clear away the extra lens you have that you have not used in the last seven years. Neither will it help you save money for the camera that you truly want. It is better to save up and buy a camera that you truly need/want rather than to sacrifice your money and hopes that this camera will help you take the perfect picture when you know that the reality of the situation is different from your imagination.

## Throw Away Broken Pieces

We all have that drawer filled with broken pieces of tech that we will never need again or even try to fix. That drawer filled with earbuds with only one ear working. It's time to throw it away. You no longer need them, buy a new pair of earbuds and get rid of the ones you no longer use. Take a look into the drawer and ask yourself if you find it beautiful? Do you find the tech you can no longer use useful?

The answer is probably no. Stop trying to reason to yourself and look for tech that will either last or have a warranty on it that will replace your purchase if it is damaged or lost. Aim for quality over quantity. Instead of having five headphones that you bought at the gas station, find a notable company that makes good headphones and invest in yourself. You may just find a pair that you find beautiful.

You can apply the rule of quality over quantity in more than one area of your life. Think about buying better quality clothes and getting rid of the other pieces that have holes in them or have become discolored with years of wear and tear.

### Consolidate

Consolidating the tech that you chose to have is a great way of limiting your impact on the earth. It can also help limit the number of times you get distracted by new tech. Use the One In, One Out rule here to help you consolidate your tech. If you get a new phone: giveaway, sell or throw away the old one. This advice goes for all your other techs as well. The only exception to the rule may be cameras, as some cameras have a certain way of portraying the world that is unique to its build. Cameras answer the question "Do you find it beautiful?" with an emphatic yes.

You can always donate your old tech to someone who needs it more than you. You may even sell it for parts online. Let the technology that you love to use help you to gain income rather than take money away from our pockets.

# Media Cleansing

What is media cleansing and where do you start?

Media Cleansing is the act of stepping away from social media in order to realign yourself with the goals that you have in life. You may have gotten distracted with the retweet from your favorite artist or the tag game that you have played for the fifth time this week and it's not even Thursday yet (Unless it is Thursday). Think of social media cleansing as getting a tech detox. You are eliminating the things from your body that may harm you when you detox with social media cleansing you are eliminating those things that may harm your psyche.

This is all for your mental health.

Taking a step away from social media can do wonders for your self-image and self-confidence. Often times we compare ourselves with what we think beauty is, we asked ourselves if we are similar to one individual or what another individual looks better compared to us. This is detrimental to our mental health; we shouldn't be comparing ourselves with another person but striving to be our best selves.

Minimalism asks the question: Do we find it beautiful?

And that is important because our concept of beauty change as we grow older. What we may have found beautiful when we are younger may have now become obsolete. If we're always updating our view of what we say beauty is, then our perspective of what true beauty is can easily be warped or changed.

You should be the only one defining your idea of beauty.

# Five Signs That You Need A Social Media Cleansing

You live for the retweets and have for a while now. Know that you are not alone, we spend entirely too much time as a society on the internet. We get lost in the likes and the new photos from that latest vacation your friend from second grade took with her family.

### 1. You lack inspiration

You have been staring at your computer for the last few days and nothing is coming to you. You pick up your phone to look at Instagram. After four hours you have yet to find inspiration, but you have liked enough photos and short videos to make your own channel. You won't find your inspiration solely by looking at others. Take a step away from the social media feed and look more into finding the things that make you feel beautiful again.

### 2. You have yet to complete your to-do list

Your to-do list has yet to be complete and that is starting to become a major problem. Put down the phone and get a better understand of why you are procrastinating. Take a few moments to get your to-do list done. Simple.

### 3. You have become indecisive

You are running behind and have lost your way. The last time you made a decision was whether to put butter on your bread and it took you 20 minutes of scrolling through your feed. Take a step back and make decisions that will help your life get better. Stop running away from your responsibilities and take a step in the direction that helps you to complete your tasks.

### 4. You are stressed out by deadlines

You have spent so much time online that your deadlines are now all tomorrow and you have only just now decided to get work done. You have procrastinated long enough. Clear out the clutter in your mind and know that you can do it. Your goals are more beautiful and important than just waiting for someone to post something online.

### 5. You are falling behind on your goals

At the beginning of the year, you set a goal and wanted to achieve a new life for yourself. Take a look into the mirror and know that you are going to be okay. You have yet to meet your fitness goals and have regressed in your thinking. Take a cleanse and got get those goals.

## Time Away From Your Television

How much time do you spend watching television each day?

What are you avoiding by spending time in front of your television?

There is a lot to get from going on without television if you're on the fence. Your capacity to think is the greatest advantage. Some individuals claim that some of their finest thoughts are done in the shower–and why the so-called' shower thoughts' is very common. This is because we have nothing but our mind to distract us literally in the shower. The water running is noisy enough to block your house's sounds. Think of the valuable' thinking moment' every single day doubling, tripling or quadrupling! When you just let her breathe, it is wonderful where your mind will go.

It is entirely up to you to decide whether or not you decide to cut the cable bill. If you don't want to. That's okay. You are not the only minimalist with television or who still has a cable bill. Remember there is no such thing as a perfect minimalist. You can take this journey any way that suits your life and goals.

## Learning About Yourself

Another big reason to let your Television go. You will rediscover your hobbies or something you like, but before you "had no time." You may discover yourself reading a book or robbing a magazine of some looks. Or the house will look boring—maybe too quiet—so you are going to come out and relax your hobby about gardening, DIY or woodwork. Or you will know that it is perfect to begin crafting again in your living room. Regardless of your hobby, when your television becomes an alternative, you will discover the energy to share.

## Increase Your Productivity

It always appears to be no brainer for me as I am so busy, but sometimes all we need is to push (or pull) to get the job done. And it's too simple to delay if there's a diversion, be it TV, cell phone, video games, etc. Distractions are all too enjoyable! Take the distraction off and your boredom will take the form of productivity.

## Save Money

One thing I hear constantly—and for many years I've been fighting for myself—is how difficult it is to save cash. By cutting our cable bill, you could have saved about $4,000 over the years.

Depending on the channel you subscribe, it could be greater. You could even be saved from $420–$1500 if you even try to cut this for a year!

# The Real Problem

We can blame our televisions all we want for infringing on our minimalistic lifestyle but the real problem here is us. If we wish to change then we must actively work with the intent to change our lives. We can't go around blaming the television and the internet for making us lazy or couch potatoes. Each day we must choose to live a minimalist lifestyle and to be present with our surroundings.

If you start thinking about how you can be absent from the things that rob you of your time and be present with the things that make you feel connected to the world around you.

Like anybody else, web addiction has become a big part of my social media cleansing. The challenge is to manage our use; therefore we don't spend our entire time behind a laptop. We depend on technology for our jobs already. Let's not let it also take over our private life.

So when you think about getting rid of your television, where will your time go when you no longer have a television to distract your thoughts.

Solve the real problem and hope to gain understanding and wisdom concerning your actions, thoughts, and deeds. If you can find beauty in learning more about yourself and those around you, then you have already won half the battle. Think about the core pillars of minimalism and how they can help you find value and beauty in meeting new people and trying new things.

Remember to place value in the people that you meet and the relationships that you are able to build. This is not to say that you will be a social butterfly, but even within your small group of people, there is importance with cherishing the meaningful connections that you are able to make.

# Chapter 6: Travel

How many bags did you pack on your last vacation?

One?

Three?

Five?

How many hours did you spend hours deciding how many swimsuits/trunks you'd need? Did you end up packing that formal dress just in case of a special occasion? What if it was raining? What if the nights were cold?

What if you fell into a large mud puddle and didn't have a way of washing out your clothes? Those are the kinds of questions that creates bags full of toiletries, piles of clothing, and ready-to-use charged gadgets (that may never get used) filling up your suitcase to the limit.

Did you really need it all?

Did you use it all?

Do you think you could have fit it into one bag?

Minimalism is swept through the globe of travel, pushing travelers as well as distant employees to sweep down their properties so that they may be fitted in one or two (mostly) bags. They have their minimal properties with pride and humility when someone asks, "Is that really all you packed?"

They brag loudly about how "freely" they now travel with nothing to weigh them down. When everything you own fits into a backpack and a single suitcase nothing feels superfluous or unnecessary. Everything has a purpose and a moment to shine when you need it the most. With less baggage, less mental baggage is a given, and you get to let go of the past in anticipation of the future and what it may bring. Minimalism is the goal, but you can march to the rhythm of your own drum, figuring out the best principles for you instead of adhering to strict rules or guidelines set forth by a consumption-driven society. You are free to choose whichever path is best for you and walking on your journey full of twists and turns.

## What is Minimalist Travel?

Minimalist travel is a form of traveling where travelers only pack their material possessions that are *absolutely necessary* and nothing more. If you can fit your entire life into a suitcase, then you're doing it right. If you can fit it into your backpack - even better.

A common example of minimalist travel: a world in which people spend an entire year on the road, living out of a single backpack. It discourages buying a souvenir in every destination for the sake of buying one to say you got it in x destination. You can just take a picture instead and you may end up keeping it longer than the souvenir. It praises multi-purpose wardrobes and tools. It seeks out efficiency, quality, and simplicity over luxury or appearance.

However, minimalism is part of a greater lifestyle and mindset change. Beyond personal belongings, the idea of minimalism promotes freedom and decisiveness, two key components of what traveling is all about.

### Why are freedom and decisiveness so intricately intertwined with minimalism?

Today's society places a lot of meaning and worth in the things we own. Our homes are a reflection of who we are, so they must be perfectly decorated. Our clothing presents us to the world as we hope to be seen, so strangers may look at us and be amazed at our own style and control of the world. We buy cars to show off our latest promotion or a raise to the world around us. We lack the ability to show our internal value and beauty, thus using material possessions to validate our worth.

At times, we place our desire for more possessions over our personal needs like love, health, passions, and growth. We accumulate so many things that our closets are overflowing, but our hearts still feel empty.

Minimalism is the first step to reversing this emptiness that eventually comes from mass consumption. It encourages people to let go of the things that are cluttering their lives with meaningless items and lean into the things that make us feel alive and truly bring us joy. It breaks the shackles that were holding us hostage to our stuff. It lets us focus on the things that are important, instead of distracting us with things that are shiny.

## How to Be a Minimalist Traveler

Minimalism can seem out of reach when you aren't sure if you'll be able to easily access necessities in locations around the world. It can be daunting knowing that everything that you're packing is all that you have. You may be heading somewhere where you won't have easy access to the items that you've grown accustomed to (your favorite shampoo or familiar breakfast cereal), but, here's the good news, you might just find a new favorite. However, once you put on your minimalist thinking cap, you'll realize that it's not about how much you bring, but which things you bring, and how you approach your traveling experience as a whole.

Let's start with the first one: what to bring. There are a million minimalist packing lists on the internet, and the main points are pretty much the same, but few are made for people who are living a nomadic lifestyle. Tweak each list to fit your personal preferences and get going. The world awaits!

## Start with a light bag

Pro tip for packing: don't let the bag itself take up most of your weight limit. Your belongings should not literally weigh you down! Whether you want to invest in a lightweight rolling suitcase or commit to a backpack-based lifestyle, make sure that you're choosing a model made out of materials that can stand the test of time, without the extra weight.

Stock up on mesh packing cubes if you're going the suitcase route. These will help you stay organized while giving you a visual on how much stuff you can actually fit in your bag. If you have to sit on it just to zip it up, you're not doing minimalism right.

## The world's (not) your runway

If you're a fashionista, this could be the most difficult part of your minimalist journey. As much as clothing provides us with energy and a way to express ourselves, it can also contribute to the problems associated with materialism and excess.

That's not to say that you can't be fashionable when you travel. To fully embrace minimalist travel, we suggest creating a capsule wardrobe. Choose a few pieces that you could wear on any occasion, and make sure that everything matches with everything.

Stick to neutrals to avoid packing something that you'll only wear once a month - on a long-term trip, those items just won't cut it. Pick materials that won't wrinkle easily. This isn't the time to get flashy. It's the time to get practical and ask yourself what you're actually going to want to wear day after day in each destination. Remember this: you'll still have access to shopping in many of the places that you travel to, so if you're going to be traveling through multiple different climates, plan on donating items as you go.

## Get techy with it

The key to choosing the right gadgets and gear for your trip is whether or not you can accomplish multiple tasks with them. A laptop? That's a must-have. A wireless mouse, keyboard and a cell phone that doubles as a hotspot? Maybe. An electric corkscrew? You might want to leave that behind.

## So fresh, so clean

Our tip for toiletries: buy them when you arrive, and only get what you need. There's no use in packing a year's worth of toothpaste for your trip or stocking up on your favorite body wash just so it can take up a ton of room in your bag. Most of your destinations will have drug stores or pharmacies where you can grab the necessities.

You could also use this travel experience to embrace a packaging-free lifestyle. Companies are starting to make plastic-free shampoo bars and planet-friendly body soaps. These items will take up less space in your bag and they're great for the environment - it's a win-win!

Think of it this way: toiletries are not the key things that bring you joy - so why would you want to take them with you from place to place? Let each city's unique vibe inspire you to try something new. You'll never know if Italian haircare is actually better unless you try it for yourself, right?

## How to Travel

Now that you're done packing, the fun part begins; the actual living. Living as a minimalist traveler is about so much more than narrowing down your belongings and holding back from buying more things. It's about investing in experiences instead of possessions, and thriving on the fact that nothing is keeping you from living the life that you want to live.

Here are some tips on how to make minimalism a core component of your travel experience:

### Edit, edit, edit

So you're three months into your travels and you realize that you've managed to accumulate some extra things along the way. It's human nature to want to find and store things that seem to be significant or have a bit of value, but when you're trying to live a minimalist style, extra stuff can be a problem. Once a month, take a look at your belongings and determine whether or not they serve a purpose for you on this trip. If the answer is no...

### ...Give a little bit

There are going to be moments when you find yourself with more than you need. Maybe your bag isn't zipping quite as easy as it used to, or you fell off the wagon and bought a pretty tapestry from a local market. It happens.

When it feels like you're ready to move on from an item, embrace the concept of radically gifting. Find a local organization that supports people in need and see if they could benefit from your item. Perhaps that woman down the street will find your tapestry just as beautiful, and it will serve her more than it does you. Every time you give something away you'll find that it gets easier and easier to do. With each gifting, you'll sense that you have less connection to material things and more of a connection to the people that you're providing with happiness.

## Seek minimalist experiences

Finally, minimalism doesn't just come down to what you own. It also relates to what you're doing. Consider following a few slow travel concepts and seek out experiences that fill you up, instead of existing as a checkmark on your bucket list. Look for activities that let you exercise the freedom that you've gained from a minimalist lifestyle, like an impromptu weekend spent on an island or a trek to a campsite in the Sahara. You'll find that spontaneity is abundant when you don't have to worry about leaving your things behind.

Connect with the people that you meet along the way, and let them get to know you for who you really are, instead of the "you" that your possessions portray. Give in to the feeling that you're untethered to anything on this Earth except for your own destiny. Pursue your passions and grow with abandon now that the accumulation of things isn't a priority. Now you know what truly matters - you're just thankful that freedom doesn't take up any space in your bag.

## Traveling With Children

When you decide to travel with a minimalistic mindset remember that your children may also go along the journey with you. Traveling with children tend to tether you to the present a bit more. Look into local events that will teach your children the beauty of a different culture or the appreciation of a creative space. Teach your children the beauty and value of traveling lighter and with a minimalistic outlook on life. It will take them far in life and help them to value the presence of others and the depth of great relationships.

# Chapter 7: Optimizing Your Plate

Have you ever considered the thought that minimalism could change the way that you eat?

Well, it can!

Your plate is the next target of our worldwide domination plans. We hope to help you streamline how you cook and the way you eat to help you live a healthier life. While food is a necessity in life how we eat can vastly affect how we live. We all know that some foods are better for us than others. Yet we continue to eat how we want to hope to meet our health goals: This is a system built to fail.

It may be conscientious that to be a minimalist you have to be vegan or vegetarian or else your membership card will be revoked. This is simply not true. You don't have to eat a strictly plant-based diet to be a minimalist.

There is no perfect way to achieve minimalism; especially on your plate.

In this chapter, we want to leave you with a few tips to minimize your plate and maximize your health. We hope to leave you thinking about the way you view food and how it can affect how you eat.

## Changing Your View

Before we can optimize our plates, we must change how we think about food. Food is a delicacy meant to be enjoyed not scarf down. If we are to change how we view food must first understand why we need food and how our thoughts about food can change our own self-image. We hardly think of food a something great importance, yes we eat it when we're hungry but food is more than just for hunger. Food is meant to be celebrated and to be eaten when needed.

we overeat oftentimes not due to hunger but thirst. Part of minimalism is making sure that your body is in its optimal condition so that you can appreciate the essentials of life. Different cultures view food according to how they were raised. Treat food with respect but let us not forget that it is supposed to provide the nutrients that we need in order to survive.

If you want to apply minimalistic principles to what you eat then be sure to ask the three questions.

## Does it add value to my life?

Think about your macros here. If you have never heard about Macros, it is short for Macronutrients. Which can be broken down into three major categories: Fat, Protein, and Carbs. By setting a limit to how much fat, protein, and carbs you can have you will be able to better maintain your health.

A common percentage to go with for your macros is 35% Protein, 30% Carbs, and 35% Fat for maintenance. There are several apps that can help you stay within your macros and help you either lose, gain, or maintain your weight on a journey to a healthier you.

## Do I find it beautiful?

Food can look really beautiful especially when you get a bit creative with how you put it together. A colorful salad or dressing your dish as if you were at a five-star restaurant. Take time to make your food beautiful and enjoy each bite. No matter what your dietary needs are, you can enjoy a delicious and colorful salad.

## Does it grant me freedom?

There are so many people who feel like they are a prisoner to food. They are only allowed such freedoms when it comes to certain types of foods and that can be few and far in-between. If you have bad gut health and need to reset your cut bacteria, there are plenty of dietary changes that we can make that will help our digestive system.

Finding the right eating plan for you may some take time but it will allow you to feel better and live a healthy life.

## Grocery Shopping Made Simple
### MAKE A LIST AND STICK TO IT!!!!

Grocery shopping should not be a hassle but it often times is. To minimize your stress try planning out your meals for the week and shop according to the ingredients that you will need to prepare those meals and you will be able to minimize random purchases.

Aim to buy fresh vegetables and check your local grocery store for different sales to see how they compare to what you have in mind for the week. This does not mean drive to five different stores just to see what their fresh produce is like; it means learning to do without certain things that you have grown accustomed to.

Learning to reduce your grocery list to the essentials, this is not saying that you can't have a treat or delicious foods. As long as you plan out what you are going to eat for the week or month, it will make grocery shopping so much more efficient.

Prepping Like a Pro

Food Prepping is one of the simplest things you can do to make your life simpler. Achieving a minimalistic plate is more about how you prep than what you eat. We believe that careful preparation leads to a simpler life in the end and that's our hope to live minimally and free. To be able to travel or have a place to call home

# Chapter 8: A Steady Minimalist Mind

In much the way your physical space is cluttered with all the things you have collected throughout your life, your mind is cluttered with all the baggage hanging around from your past experiences. Practicing mindfulness will help you push all of that to the side so that you find a quiet mental space to let yourself simply be for a little while. While sitting in silence for a few minutes might not seem like it can accomplish much, if you give it a try for a full month you will be shocked at the difference it can make.

Mindfulness meditation is a type of meditation which focuses on being as aware of each moment as possible, thereby helping the consciousness to expand by forming a stronger connection with the present. Mindfulness meditation has a long history of practice as part of the Buddhist faith where it is revered for its ability to improve both mental happiness and physical well-being. This has been corroborated by research which shows that mindfulness meditation is a beneficial treatment for a variety of mental conditions. What's more, it has also been shown to be effective when treating conditions including anxiety, stress and drug addiction.

Practicing mindfulness is a skill and like all skills can be improved with practice. To practice mindful meditation, you simply try and retain as much focus on the current moment as possible with the help of repetitive breathing and the information being relayed by the senses. Studies have shown that practicing mindfulness for just 15 minutes per day can lead to measurable results when it comes to reducing stress and improving a sense of self. This is caused in no small part by the positive effects mindfulness has on emotional regulation, attention span, and body awareness. What's more, neuroimaging results show that practicing mindfulness also helps the mind process information more effectively.

Research shows that practicing mindfulness regularly can improve brain health as well as function and starting young will ensure your brain retains more volume as you age. Those who regularly practice mindfulness will also find they have a thicker hippocampus and as a result, have an easier time learning and retaining more information. They will also notice that the part of the amygdala which controls fear, anxiety, and stress is less active. With all of these physical changes to the brain is it any wonder that those who practice mindfulness report a general increase in well-being and mood?

Beyond the physical changes, regularly practicing mindfulness has been shown to decrease instances of participant's minds getting stuck in negative thought patterns while at the same time increasing focus. This should not come as a surprise given the fact that a recent Johns Hopkins study found that regularly practicing mindfulness meditation is equally effective at treating depression, ADD and anxiety.

With so many physical and mental benefits, is it any wonder that mindfulness meditation is revered by Buddhists all around the world? The practice has its roots in a type of structured meditation called vipassana which, when translated, refers to a mental state that promotes living in the moment while still being aware of how the present and the future intertwine. Those who master vipassana are said to more fully understand the universe as a whole as well as their place in it.

In order to reach a state of vipassana, practitioners strive for what are known as the three marks of existence: impermanence, non-self, and dissatisfaction, which together are believed to bring unity to all living things. Non-self refers to the idea of understanding the boundaries between the self and the physical world with the understanding that coming to terms with these boundaries make it easier to fully grasp the intricacies of both. Meanwhile, dissatisfaction refers to the innate desire to seek satisfaction from fleeting experiences and the inevitable feeling that losing these things creates. This leads into the idea of importance as only by accepting the temporary nature of life can true happiness and inner peace be found.

## Other reasons to practice mindfulness meditation

Mindfulness meditation naturally leads to a deeper understanding of the self and allows many people to take stock of their strengths and weaknesses, leading to personal growth.

Studies show that those who practice mindfulness regularly have a stronger memory, leading to easier retention of facts in both the long and the short term.

In addition to the specifics, mindfulness meditation improves overall physical wellbeing with those who practice regularly reporting fewer instances of illness and a more rapid recovery when they do fall ill.

Mindfulness meditation can help improve emotional control while at the same time increasing one's threshold for pain.

As surprising as it might seem, making a habit of being mindful can actually make even the most middling music seem more engaging. This deeper level of engagement leads to a general increase of enjoyment, regardless of the type of music or any previous musical preferences.

## Getting started with mindfulness meditation

While more fully connecting with every moment might sound like something that is beyond your ken, the fact of the matter is that once you commit the practice of mindfulness meditation to habit, the improved state will come to you quite quickly. What's more, once you understand the basics you will likely find that you can practice mindfulness meditation virtually anywhere as long as you can commit to being fully in the present and listening to the things your body is telling you.

While mindfulness meditation is exceedingly malleable, when you are first starting out you should set aside at least 15 minutes a day in a place that is free of distractions in order to start seeing benefits as quickly as possible. The space you choose should be somewhere you can feel truly relaxed and not have to worry about anything. As mindfulness meditation is all about getting in touch with yourself and the signals your body is sending you starting off with the fewest number of external stimuli is the preferable choice.

### Form a routine

The easiest way to transition the act of mindfulness meditation into a habit is to start by making it part of your daily routine. As with any of the new habits discussed in these pages, letting your mind and body get used to the practice and expect it at the same time every day is crucial to keeping it around long enough for it to become a habit. As practicing mindfulness meditation requires nothing special and the benefits will not be immediately apparent, many people find it easy to make excuses to not practice regularly.

If you find that you are constantly coming up with excuses not to meditate then you will want to remember the ancient mindfulness saying which goes something like, "practice mindfulness meditation for 15 minutes per day; unless, of course, your schedule is very full in which case you will want to practice for 30 minutes." Don't use the outside world to make excuses that affect your potential for inner peace, find a few spare minutes each day and commit to doing so for 30 days, at the end of this time you will be glad you stuck with it.

## Start small

For just a few minutes, take a seat. It need not be in a chair, nor do you need to sit with your legs positioned in a specific way. Simply sit down with your back straight. Put your hands in your lap and close your eyes. Then, breathe slowly. When you do, focus all of your attention on how breathing itself feels. Really fixate on the senses: the air entering and exiting your nostrils or mouth; the expansion of your lungs, how cold or warm the air is. You are just focusing on how you currently are, and not on how you can change your breath. If you notice that you are controlling your breathing, let it go. It will be tricky when you first start, so try not to focus on whether your breath is natural or not.

As you are in your seat and meditating, you will find that thoughts will pop up. There will be times that you will have several thoughts overlapping one another. These may be plans, memories, TV commercial jingles, or fantasies. You may feel like you can't even focus on your breath because of your thoughts. This is a common occurrence, especially with people that are new to meditation. The important thing is to notice how you feel. When these few minutes are up, open your eyes and examine how you feel physically and mentally. Try this once a day, extending the time a little bit each day.

Meditating in this way keeps your thoughts on something in the present. With your focal point defined you can keep coming back to it as you feel intrusive thoughts approaching. Though in this example we used breathing as our "anchor," you can focus on any sort of continuous sensation. Classically people have used the ring of a bell or the gong. They "follow" the sound until it's gone, meditating until the sound fully dissipates. You may also choose to use your physical surroundings as your focal point. If you're sitting in a chair you can focus your attention on how it feels against your body (but don't make yourself uncomfortable!).

Regardless of what method you choose for yourself, your focus point should be something that you can bring your attention back to should you get distracted. It may be difficult at first, which is why it's recommended that you start meditation for only a few minutes a day, but over time it can become as habitual as the negative thoughts you're replacing. And even though you start by practicing once a day each day, the eventual goal is to be able to meditate as needed throughout the day. It's to be used on a daily basis and on an as needed basis.

## Other ways to practice mindfulness

Perhaps the best part of mindfulness meditation is that it can be practiced just about anywhere. Unlike many types of meditation, you don't need to set aside time specifically to do it and instead can take any period of time where your body is occupied in a simple, repetitive activity.

Do chores mindfully: While typically, household chores offer up little but daily drudgery, if you approach them with the idea that they can be a pathway to enlightenment you can help yourself see them in a whole new light. When it comes to practicing mindfulness in their midst, focus on each moment as it passes, take the time to clear your mind and let it be drawn to the way your hands feel while going through the motions. Make sure you focus on the smells, sights, and sounds and as you finish take a special moment to consider how much improved your space is now that it is clean.

Shower mindfully: Showering is another task that most people only complete on autopilot. Engage in the moment, practice mindfulness meditation as you go through the ritual of cleaning yourself. Shower time is typically a feast for the senses as there is something to occupy them all. Take the opportunity to really feel and notice these things and you will start or finish the day in a more mindful place.

Exercise mindfully: The brainwaves of those who are exercising are surprising similar to those who are meditating so it is only natural to combine the two for better results. This is an ideal time to focus on the senses as your body most likely has plenty to tell you while you are putting it through its paces. Take special care to focus on the smells and sights and how your body is responding to the stimuli all around you.

# Chapter 9: Clearing Your Mental Clutter

In order to set your mind up for mindfulness success in the long-term, it is important that you do everything you can to clear out your mental space just as you did your physical space.

## The threat of Cognitive Distortions

What are Cognitive distortions? They're negative thought patterns and exaggerated thoughts that you believe to be reality. Sometimes they even pop into your head subconsciously. Recognizing distorted thoughts is the first step in changing them.

### Filtering

This type of cognitive distortion makes you focus on the negative, and ignoring the positive. For example, you were let go from your job because your company is losing money. Naturally, all you can think about is that you need to find a new job as soon as possible. But your distortions start to intensify and all you can think about is how you're not good enough. You don't even consider that maybe you didn't enjoy working at that company anyways or that it's your chance to turn your hobby into a career.

Ask yourself, Do I tend to ignore all the good things going for you and focus on the bad? Do I forget about the good things that happened in the day and let the negative thing take over?

### Overgeneralization

When you have this type of cognitive distortion, you assume all experiences and people are the same. For example, you agree to go on a date with someone you met online. The date goes horribly and from here on out, you assume that dating is not for you. Everyone you meet online is probably a bad person.

Ask yourself, Do I always feel that the same stressful situations are likely to occur more than once? Do I assume that the bad experiences will repeat and bad people are always the same?

## Polarized thinking

When you have this type of cognitive distortion, you only think in black and white. There is no grey area. For example, you fail your driving test. You think that you're never going to be able to drive and give up on driving.

Ask yourself, Do I base all experiences on one bad experience? Do I think that when things go bad there is nothing that can go right again?

## Jumping to Conclusions

When you have this type of cognitive distortion, you let negative take over and convince you with little evidence. For example, you tell a joke at a party and no one laughs, you immediately think that everyone thinks you're stupid.

Ask yourself. Do I jump to conclusions? Do I believe in my negative thoughts without considering the opposite?

## Catastrophizing

When this type of cognitive distortion occurs, you automatically think of all the worst-case scenarios. For example, you text your significant other, but they don't reply right away. And you start to believe that he's cheating on you.

Ask yourself: When I'm in a stressful situation, do I immediately magnify the negative and make it seem way worse than it is?

## Personalization

When this type of cognitive distortion occurs, you immediately think the stressful situation is your fault. For example, you were late to an important dinner, you think to yourself that if only you had planned better and told your significant other to hurry up that you would've been on time.

Ask yourself: Do I blame myself when I'm anxious? Do I take everything personally? Do I think that people are working against me? Am I always the cause of unhealthy relationships?

## Control Fallacies

Similar to personalization, this type of cognitive distortion occurs when you think everything that happens to you is your fault. But there is a slight difference. Control fallacies are about feeling like you have a lack of control over your life. Stressful situations happen and you think you're to blame or others are to blame. For example, you always think your partner isn't happy because of something you did.

Ask yourself: Do I think there's no point to do something because it's your fault or someone else's fault?

## Fallacy Fairness

When this type of cognitive distortion occurs, you are obsessed with the fairness of stressful situations. For example, you're torn between two friends who are at odds and you feel resentful because you think you know what to do, but no one is listening.

Ask yourself, Am I over concerned with what's fair and what isn't? Does contemplating the fairness of stressful situations make me feel angry, hopeless or depressed? Do I always think I know what's fair, but other people don't?

## Blaming

When this type of cognitive distortion occurs, you think other people are to blame for your emotional pain. For example, you think it's your coworkers' fault for the presentation not going the way it was intended.

Ask yourself, Do I think other people are making me feel bad about myself?" "Do I think other people are out to get me?

## Shoulds

When this type of cognitive distortion occurs, you live your life following should and must statements and you feel sadness or anger when you break these statements or When directed at other people who break these statements. For example, every time you miss a gym session, you think to yourself how horrible you feel and that you shouldn't be so lazy.

Ask yourself, do force myself into a should statement like I should go to the gym', but when I don't go, I feel terrible? Do I have personal should statements for my friends like "My friends should know when to call me" that they don't know about and I get mad when they break them?

## Emotional Reasoning

When this type of cognitive distortion occurs, you think that the way you feel makes the negative statement true. For example, you feel foolish for falling for a prank, so you automatically think that maybe it is because you are a foolish person.

Ask yourself: When I feel negative, do I believe that negative feeling is true? Do I think that what I feel means that it's reality?

## Fallacy of Change

When this type of cognitive distortion occurs, you rely on other people to change and suit your needs --Your happiness depends on others. For example, you think you'd be happier if your significant other would change the way they dressed or offered you more time.

Ask yourself, Do I think that if someone else changes, it will make me happier?

## Global Labelling

When this type of cognitive distortion occurs, you clump and generalize negative instances into one negative judgement about themselves or other people. For example, when you encounter stressful situations that you failed at, you think to yourself "I'm stupid".

Ask yourself "Do I overgeneralize when I or someone else fails and give myself or them an unhealthy label?"

## Always Right

When this type of cognitive distortion occurs, you believe that being wrong is unacceptable and you'll go to lengths to prove that you know what's right. You'll put other people on trial to prove their opinions are wrong. For example, you think that arguing your point of view is always the right thing to do, no matter whose feelings you hurt. And how damaged the relationship will be.

Ask yourself, Do I always need to be right? Do I hurt people in the process? Do I hurt the ones I care by being overtly honest and challenging them?

## Heaven's Reward Fallacy

When this type of cognitive distortion occurs, you are convinced that any well doing on your part will be a reward. This is a false belief. There is no one keeping score and when your sacrifice isn't met with a reward, you feel angry and bitter. For example, you think that by working your lunch hours away, your boss will think that you're working hard and you'll eventually be rewarded.

Ask yourself, Do I always feel that there's some higher being that I'm answering too and this higher being is keeping score?

Now that you're familiar with the 15 cognitive distortions, you'll probably know which distortions you tend to engage in. Our brains are powerful engines and naturally wired to link ideas, concepts, and actions together. But sometimes negative associations become part of the wiring. This can develop from the way you grew up, or because of the bad habits you've picked up. And when you blindly believe in these fallacies, it adds fuel to the fire that becomes emotional pain. It's time to challenge those distortions. Now, you can move on to the next step, cognitive restructuring. Cognitive restructuring is the core part of CBT, it helps you reframe cognitive distortions by identifying them. In the next chapter, you'll find 12 strategies commonly used in cognitive restructuring to help you overcome stress, panic, anxiety, and worry.

## What to do about it

The next step in your mental decluttering journey is to challenge the distortions you have. You must take an active role in your journey or nothing will change. Push beyond your comfort zone when you can without throwing yourself in the deep end. There are 12 strategies outlined in this book for you to practice. Remember that this process isn't an easy one. You are going against what has been ingrained in you over many years and rewiring the way your brains works. The first few attempts at these exercises will be difficult. It'll feel like you're going nowhere. Trust the process. The more you practice, the easier it'll get, and the better you'll feel. Also, keep in mind that these strategies are meant to be revisited as often as you can and as often as you like.

## Strategy 1—Thought Tracking

We all have thoughts that seem to pop up out of nowhere and we don't question them. We just believe them. These random thoughts are "automatic thoughts". They can be good or bad thoughts, but when they're distortions, you'll find that you'll "randomly" start feeling anxious and worrisome. Don't let these subconscious distortions slip--start noticing them. Spend a couple of days noticing automatic thoughts.

Negative automatic thoughts have no weight nor evidence to support the distortion. They're fleeting moments that leave a negative impact in your mood. The only way to stop them is to start noticing them and writing them down. Recognize that these automatic thoughts are nothing but baseless projections. If you're having trouble deciphering whether an automatic thought is a distortion or not, ask yourself this:

1. Does the automatic thought have evidence to prove its validity?
2. Is the automatic thought an opinion or fact?

If you're still unsure take a look at these examples of what negative automatic thoughts can sound like.

Example
Situation: You raised your hand to answer a question, but answered incorrectly. The thought "I'm stupid" pops up and it immediately ruins your day. The thought may go away, but it doesn't make your day any better.

This statement is an opinion and has no real evidence to prove that it's right. And not knowing one question doesn't make anyone stupid.

Example
Situation: You go to a friend's party and start to feel anxious. The thought "everyone is judging me" pops in and keeps you from interacting with others.
This statement is an opinion. It's a negative reaction to what your experiencing at the party.

Example
Situation: As you grab your coffee, you accidentally spill some hot coffee on the person next to you. You think "That was clumsy of me."
This statement is a fact because it refers to a specific event that happened and is not generalized. You are not always clumsy, but that specific event was, in fact, a clumsy move.

Let's dive deeper into the thought tracking strategy now that you are familiar with automatic distorted thoughts. The beauty of this strategy is that you can do this anywhere. But to start off, let's put words on papers, so you can reread the process. Grab a pen and paper, find a seat and let's work on a distorted thought. Follow these simple steps to break down and reframe negativity.

Step 1: Identify the adversity. Go into as much or as little detail as you'd like, and try to answer these questions. What happened? What's causing your negative thought? Is it an event or something that someone said?

Step 2: Identify the negative thought. If there are more than one, put it on a different page. Work through each thought one at a time.

Step 3: Write down your feelings about negative thoughts. Write about how that negative thought made you feel and why you would believe in it.

Step 4: Repute these thoughts. Stand up for yourself. Give reasons why you shouldn't feel the way. Do these thoughts actually have evidence? Are there other ways of looking at the distortion? Are you biased in any way?

Is your belief in the distortion useful to you in anyway? What are the implications of the experience that caused you to feel this way? What can you learn from it?

Step 5: Create a new balanced thought. You've got 2 sides of the story now. One side being the negative distorted thought and the other side of being positive. Rewrite your negative thought to change your experience. Pull from your list of positives in Step 4.

Your thought tracking exercise should look something like this example.

Step 1: Identify the adversity
I had an important presentation today and instead of being calm and collected, I started to get nervous. When it was my turn to present, I felt like I wasn't ready and fumbled on every slide. People even laughed at me and I turned red from embarrassment.

Step 2: Identify the negative thought.

I'm terrible at my job. (Let's use this negative thought in step 3)

I'm not good enough for the company.

I suck.

Note: You can list out as many as you like but move forward one thought at a time.

Step 3: Write down your feelings about the negative thought.

It makes me feel sad and unworthy. I feel like I don't deserve the job and other people probably think that as well. It's embarrassing to suck this much.

Step 4: Repute these thoughts.

Well, I guess practice makes perfect. I haven't done a lot of presentations yet, so it only makes sense that I would fumble so bad. I've got bad nerves that will probably go away with more practice and exposure. Maybe I'm too hard on myself because I'm still new to this experience. They say you learn every time you fall so maybe next time; I'll prepare more to make sure I don't fumble again.

Step 5: Create a new balanced thought.

My one bad presentation doesn't mean I'm terrible at my job. It's a learning experience and it doesn't define my abilities. I learn from my mistakes in the past so I can prepare for the future. This presentation is only a steppingstone to many more great presentations I'll give. No one is perfect.

Thought tracking is a quick and easy way to reframe your thinking. It forces you to consider the alternatives to a stressful situation. There are always two sides to the story and thought tracking makes it clear that we don't have to tell ourselves the negative side of the story. We grow and develop through the positive sides.

## Strategy 2—Exposure

Exposure is a great strategy for those who encounter anxiety and fear with things, activities, or situations. Some common psychological fears that exposure therapy has helped with is social anxiety, PTSD and panic disorders. The main purpose of exposure is as the name suggests, expose you to those things and situations over and over again to reduce the negative thought. The theory is that when we avoid things, we start to fear them more. Avoidance increases our anxiety to the point where the anxiety and fear will have been worse than it really is. By systematically exposing yourself to stressful situations or things, you'll learn to reframe your negative thoughts. You'll learn that there is nothing to fear and the changes in your thinking can be lasting.

Let's start by making a list of situations or things that cause anxiety. Pinpoint those moments. If you've been journaling, you can look back at your journal to help you find those moments. Try and be as specific as possible, so that you can replicate the scenario and practice exposing yourself to it.

Example

I get too anxious when talking to people at parties, so I avoid them.
Or
I am extremely afraid of public speaking. When I present, I let my team talk.

There are different ways you can practice exposure depending on your fear and anxieties. Take one of your fears or anxieties and try any of these exposure techniques to get started.

In Vivo Exposure forces you to directly face your feared object, activity, or situation. For example, if you feel anxious speaking in public in front of so many people, try putting yourself in front of crowds more. Start taking small steps to speaking in front of more than one person, two people, 3 people, and work your way up. You can find opportunities like this in your community where circles of people share their own writings and they must read their creative work in front of people. Push yourself a little further each time or throw yourself in the deep end and join a comedy club.

Imaginal Exposure forces you to vividly imagine your feared, object, activity, or situation. This is a great technique for people who have PTSD and for situations that can't be replicated. For example, ask yourself to recall vividly a traumatic memory or experience. Recall every detail aloud or on paper to yourself and keep revisiting the memory to reduce the negative thoughts and feelings.

Interoceptive Exposure forces you bring on the sensations of fear to learn that fear and anxiety sensations are harmless. This is a great technique for anyone with a panic disorder. Intense fear of something may force you to fear that fear sensation where your body heats up and goes into a fight or flight mode. For example, for those who fear the feeling of panic itself, they may avoid any situation that makes their heartbeat fast. They can try raising their heart beats in a controlled environment so that they learn to accurately judge their environment.

Virtual Reality Exposure forces you to face your fears in virtual reality. It's contained and versions of In Vivo Exposure and is used when object, activities, and situations aren't practical to recreate. For example, someone who is afraid of taking the airplane can be forced to virtually sit on an airplane or play airplane related games to fight the fear.

As your attempt to expose yourself to new experiences find ways to associate positive moments to the experience to change your outlook of the feared object, activity, or situation. And take baby steps at first, but always remember to keep pushing your boundaries once you feel comfortable facing the fear. The more you avoid the fear, the greater the fear becomes. The avoidance can generalize to other areas of your life creating more things to fear. It eats you up.

## Strategy 3 — Behavioral Activation

Do you ever feel like you just want to stay home because you're not in the mood? And then you end up feeling terrible after sleeping the whole day and depressed that you wasted your time? Behavioral activation is exactly what you need. This strategy helps you increase behaviors that you should be doing more by scheduling them ahead of time.

Depressive moods can isolate you by decreasing your motivations to seek rewarding activities. When you've been isolated for a long time, you'll start to lose your sense of well-being which pulls you down deeper into a dark depressive mood. By identifying when this happens, you can start planning ahead of time to avoid your aversion behavior.

There's a reason why when you feel unmotivated and isolate yourself when you're depressed. It's a natural response from your brain to avoid things that may hurt you. Your brain's natural response to your depressive mood is to protect. That means that the more you isolate yourself and listen to the brain, the less your brain will be likely to change. The theory behind behavioral activation is that you must do the opposite of what your brain is telling you to do in order to activate the feeling of motivation. But, why activate first? This is because it changes the way your brain. Activations can be exercising or simply going for a walk when you don't want to. This is why behavioral activation is especially effective for people who don't engage in rewarding activities because of depression or have difficulty finishing tasks because of procrastination. Behavioral activation helps end the vicious cycle that many people with anxiety, fear, and depression fall into.

Let's try and understand this vicious cycle more. There are actually 2 vicious cycles that intensifies depression. Once you fall into the first one, you usually fall into the second one as well if nothing is done.

This is the first vicious cycle:

Event → Negative Emotions → Negative Actions.

An event or negative memory triggers negative emotions that are distressing. Because of how distressing the negative emotions are, it usually leads to avoidance and isolation behaviors. This is the first cycle. If no action is taken to improve mood and disposition, then a second cycle will usually be encountered

This is the second vicious cycle:

First vicious cycle → Event → Negative Emotions ⇄ Negative Actions.

In the second vicious cycle, the negative actions lead and or cause another distressing even that again leads to negative emotions and negative actions. These isolation behaviors usually make you feel even worse because you haven't engaged in any rewarding tasks. Continuing to engage in negative actions will eventually lead to the start of the second vicious cycle. And similar to the first cycle, if no action is taken, the cycle will keep on going. Take a look at the example below to understand the process more.

Example

First Vicious Cycle

Event: I lost my job at the wrong time. I'm unemployed and my wife just had our third child.

→ Negative Emotions: I'm embarrassed, anxious, and depressed. How am I going to take care of my family?

→ Negative Actions: I'm so embarrassed and sad that I don't know what to do. I just want to hide away. I can't face anyone.

Second Vicious Cycle

First vicious cycle → Event: Because I've been shutting myself out, I haven't returned calls from friends. I missed out on so many get togethers that my friends stopped inviting me.

→ Negative Emotions: I'm sad that my friends would give up on me. Maybe I'm not worthy enough to have friends.

⇄ Negative Actions: Since I've got no support from my friends, what's the point in calling them back. I'll just keep to myself and avoid them.

See how a small setback can spiral into a larger problem? This vicious cycle never ends unless you take the initiative to change it.

Be aware of your actions and what you're doing to feed your negative thoughts. Try filling out this simple vicious cycle for yourself to see where you can start motivating yourself.

Once you've realized when you need motivators, try to schedule rewarding activities. This strategy is one of the simplest to accomplish. Pick up a hobby or anything you'd like to do and monitor your moods and make an effort to go. This can be a simple gym membership where you hold yourself accountable to go or work with a trainer who holds you accountable. You can also start picking up on new hobbies like painting, biking, knitting, cooking.

Here's a short list to get the ball rolling.

- Try a new cuisine
- Try new restaurants
- Go for a run
- Pick up some painting materials to paint your feelings away
- Book a trainer and workout with someone
- Try a workout you've never tried before like yoga, animal flow, karate, barre
- Learn a new life skill like swimming, cooking, knitting, sewing
- Connect with an old friend
- Go birdwatching
- Pick up a new instrument
- Read a new book
- Travel and experience a different culture
- Join meetups in your area

## Strategy 4—Play the Script 'til The End

If you're into theatre then this CBT strategy may be perfect for you. Play the script 'til the end gets your imagination fired up by making you examine what the worst-case scenarios would be if you believe your negative thoughts. It's a fun technique that you can practice over and over again to remind yourself that whatever happens will be okay.

This strategy can also help you identify underlying fears. You may find that you'll find irrational fears hidden in your imagined scenarios. The imagined scenarios usually reveal a core fear that you can use different strategies to work on.

Step 1: Identify the situation that worries you. Go into detail about the situation. Write down your fears and what you did or would do.

Step 2: What's the worst-case scenario? Now ask yourself if all of your worries came true in step 1 what would happen? Again, go into detail about what you imagine would happen and how you would feel. Repeat this step as many times as you'd like to draw out the worst of the worst situations.

Step 3: Now ask yourself, is your worst-case scenario actually believable? Find the biases in your stories. Is there even a likelihood of this situation happening? Try and prove why all your most feared situations wouldn't actually happen.

Take a look at this short example to get an idea of how this strategy works.

Step 1: I'm worried I didn't study enough for my final exam. What if I don't pass?

Step 2: If I don't pass this exam, I will fail my program. I will fail my family and friends. I'll never be able to catch up again which means I'll never be able to graduate. If I don't graduate, I'll be uneducated. I'll never find a job, never be successful in life.

Which means I'll live in poverty for the rest of my life. No one will want to be my friend because I'm stupid and poor.

Step 3: Maybe I am being too negative and unconfident, I've studied for weeks for this exam. Even if I do fail my family and friends would never turn their backs on me and there are plenty of dropouts who made it big. I just need to believe in myself more. The likelihood of me failing life may not be the most believable.

Enjoy this fun thought experiment. At the end of each exercise, you should realize that over dramatization of events would not have a likelihood of happening. Rewriting your worst-case scenarios should show you that everything will turn out okay no matter how bad you think things will get.

## Strategy 5 — Fact Vs. Opinion

Sometimes when you're in a negative mood, your negative thoughts become muddled. The lines start to blur between what is fact and what is an opinion. It's easy to get lost in your thoughts and common to be confused over what's fact and an opinion. This simple labelling exercise is extremely easy to complete and used widely because it gets straight to the point. While completing the exercise you'll immediately see that all your negative thoughts are not necessarily true.

What is a Fact?
A fact has evidence. It has something you can grasp, see, touch, data. There is always truth behind the fact and cannot be disputed. There's nothing that can influence it being true or not because it's rational.

What's an Opinion?
An opinion is based on a belief and personal view. It can be swayed to be more true or less true. Any thought that can be

argued like this is considered an opinion. More often than not, an opinion is driven by emotion. When you're in a distressing situation, you will have your own interpretation of the situation and your negative thoughts will most likely be opinions.

To start off, let's do a practice round. Label each statement as opinion or fact.

I'm stupid.
I'm useless.
I failed the test.
I'm late for work.
My boss gave me a bad review.
I'm always right.
I should have been able to pass the test.
Everything I do I mess up at.
I'm selfish.
My boss was rude to me.
I'm not attractive.
I can't be loved.
My friend didn't like my attitude.
I spread rumors about my friend.
There's something wrong with me.

Answer: Op, Op, Fa, Fa, Fa, Op, Op, Op, Op, Fa, Op, Op, Fa, Fa, Op

Now it's your turn to challenge your own negative thoughts. Write down a list of negative thoughts that you've experienced and label them one by one. If you struggle to label them remember that facts have evidence and opinions don't. To give those labels more weight, you can give a reason for each label. Write down why you consider it a fact or opinion and why opinions should be taken lightly like guesses.

Example

I can't do anything right at work. (Opinion) - This is an opinion because I can't measure it or find evidence for it. It's just a personal opinion that I've put emotional weight on because of events that made it seem like I can't do anything right.

Once you realize that your negative thoughts are just personal opinions that can be influenced by culture, age, and more, you'll see that those negative opinions don't hold much value.

## Strategy 6 — Nightmare Exposure and Rescripting

Nightmare exposure and rescripting is a great strategy for those who are affected by nightmares induced by anxiety. It's a technique that helps you regain control over bad dreams. When nightmares feel like reality, they trigger real life responses that can carry onto conscious thoughts. Feeling real fear and anxiety during critical rest time affects all parts of your waking life and can even trigger other fears and anxiety. When you don't get the proper amount of rest for your brain and body it's more likely for you to be vulnerable to more anxious thoughts.

Your nightmares can be made less fearful by confronting the fears--This is nightmare exposure and it's the first part of the exercise. The second part of the exercise will require you to rescript the nightmare. We can't change what happens in your lives, but one thing we can change is how we tell them. And it's exactly the point of rescripting your nightmares. The purpose of nightmare exposure and rescripting is to reframe the fear and anxiety you experience by rewriting the story.

Step 1: Identify your worst fears in your nightmares.

Go into detail about what happens, where you are, how you feel and etc. Write it like a story and try to answer all the who, what, when, where, why, and how. If you're a more visual person, you can also draw it out like a comic book strip.

Step 2: Identify the emotions.
What do you feel during the nightmare? And what are the physical sensations during and when you wake up from the nightmares?

Step 3: Rewrite the feeling of that moment.
What would you like to feel in that same nightmare moment? Reframe and change your associations in that nightmare.

Step 4: Rewrite the story.
How does the worst moment need to change for you to feel comfortable? Turn your nightmare into another genre. Make it funny or sappy or romantic or adventurous. Exercise your imagination because there are no limits. Your job here is to recreate the nightmare to something you enjoy.

Here is a short example of what your exercise should look like.

Step 1: On the morning of an important interview. I wake up late. I had forgotten to set my alarm clock. I rush out the door without to make it on time but realize I'm wearing tattered clothing. I rush out to the subway either way. To my luck, the subway is out of service. So, I decide to walk. I realize I'm not going to make it and start to panic because it's the job I've always wanted.

Step 2: During the worst part of the nightmare, I often feel like I'm about to hyperventilate. My heart thumps and I feel scared. I feel like I'm lagging behind and just getting by in life because I'm not prepared.

Step 3: In the worst moment, I wish I could stay calm and collected to think of a better way to get to the interview. I wish I could stop for a minute to breathe and think to make better choices than just trudge on through.

Step 4: On the morning of an important interview. I wake up late. I rush out of the house only to realize that I'm wearing tattered clothes. The good thing is that there's a super trendy clothing store right beside where I'm interviewing. If I call a cab right now, I'll have enough time to change then go to my interview!

## Strategy 7 — Behavioral Experiments

A lot of the negative thoughts that occur are usually not true. They're projections that are intensified by emotions. We don't realize this and take it for face value without understanding why these negative thoughts are coming through. In cases like this where you can't decipher whether your negative thoughts then behavioral experiments may be the way to go at it.

A behavioral experiment is especially powerful for people who suffer from social anxieties, general anxieties, low self-esteem, and depression. It forces you to dispel your overestimations and exaggerations by testing out your theories. If you remember your science projects and experiments from your grade 8 science class, these experiments will be similar. Like science, you should never jump to conclusions without a proper experiment.

Let's start by planning the experiment.

Step 1: State your purpose

Be clear about why you are doing this experiment. This experiment isn't for fun and games it's for you to realize something. What that is, is to be determined by you.

Step 2: State what you want to test

What negative thoughts and beliefs are you trying to test and predict the outcome. Then give each outcome a prediction rating from 0-100. 0 meaning the negative thought and prediction won't come true. 100 meaning the negative thought and prediction will come true.

Step 3: State the alternate prediction

Instead of a negative prediction, what other predictions can there be. Think of a positive one, an opposite from your negative prediction. Then rate its prediction accuracy from 0-100.

Step 4: Design the experiment

What will you do to test the negative thought? How will it work and how long will it take? Will it be done with someone or will you go rogue? Be as specific as possible and there are no boundaries-- Be creative.

Step 5: Identify the challenges

Set your experiment at an appropriate comfort level to start. In this step, try to identify problems you may run into then solve or figure out an alternative way to deal with them.

Example

Step 1: State your purpose

The purpose of this experiment is to see if my anxieties about not being cool enough to go to parties is true.

Step 2: State what you want to test

I want to know if anyone will be interested in talking to me. My prediction is that no one will want to talk to me because I'm boring and lame. Rating=95

Step 3: State the alternate prediction

My alternate prediction is that I will be able to make friends because everyone has these kinds of anxieties, plus I can try and keep up the conversation by talking about the biggest movie that's out right now. It's my favorite movie and I'm sure everyone will have watched it. Rating=35

Step 4: Design the experiment

I'll attempt to go to a party and force myself to stay for at least 2 hours. I won't be a wallflower, instead, I'll try talking to new people.

Step 5: Identify the challenges

I might get too nervous to start a conversation with someone I have never met. Maybe I'll think up topics beforehand so I'm prepared to make conversation.

This is just a short version of what your behavioral experiment can look like. Your experiments may be longer and more detailed. Once you've completed the planning process, take action! Carry out your experiment to the fullest without letting your anxieties sabotage yourself. During the experiment notice your thoughts, feelings, and behaviors.

After the experiment, you'll need to evaluate your findings. Follow these steps to journal your experience and your learnings so you can read it later on as reminders.

Step 1: Reflect and observe

Write down what happened. Answer all the who, what, when, where, and whys. Don't forget to write down the positives as well. If you can, try to attach a positive to your negative finding.

Step 2: Learnings

Write down what you've learned. Are there any breakthroughs? Was there anything you did that changed your mind about the situation and the experience?

Step 3: Rate your predictions again

Go back and rewrite step 2 and 3. Give a rating to how strongly you believe in them now that you have new experiences.

Example

Step 1: Reflect and observe

I went to the part and it was hard to talk to people at first, but people were so nice and actually wanted to hear about my day. I got too nervous at one point and started to stand in a corner by myself, but someone I had talked to earlier came over and offered me a drink. Someone gave me a cold shoulder during the party, but that's okay I made friends at the party anyways.

Step 2: Learnings

I am capable of making friends. People do think I'm funny and cool when I talk about things, I'm passionate about. I am able to enjoy parties.

Step 3: Rate your predictions again

I want to know if anyone will be interested in talking to me. My prediction is that no one will want to talk to me because I'm boring and lame. Rating=95 45

My alternate prediction is that I will be able to make friends because everyone has these kinds of anxieties, plus I can try and keep up the conversation by talking about the biggest movie that's out right now. It's my favorite movie and I'm sure everyone will have watched it. Rating=35 60

Take a look at your journal and see where you can apply this strategy to change your frame of mind.

# Conclusion

Thanks for making it through to the end of *Minimalism & Decluttering Learn Secret Strategies on Living a Minimalist Lifestyle For Your House, Digital Whereabouts, Family Life & Your Own Mindset! Declutter Your Life For Finding Inner Happiness!*, let's hope it was informative and able to provide you with all of the tools you need to achieve your goals, whatever it is that they may be. Just because you've finished this book doesn't mean there is nothing left to learn on the topic, and expanding your horizons is the only way to find the mastery you seek.

Now that you have made it to the end of this book, you hopefully have an understanding of how to get started putting the concept of minimalism into practice in your life, as well as a strategy or two, or three, that you are anxious to try for the first time. Before you go ahead and start giving it your all, however, it is important that you have realistic expectations as to the level of success you should expect in the near future.

While it is perfectly true that some people experience serious success right out of the gate, it is an unfortunate fact of life that they are the exception rather than the rule. What this means is that you should expect to experience something of a learning curve, especially when you are first figuring out what works for you. This is perfectly normal, however, and if you persevere you will come out the other side better because of it. Instead of getting your hopes up to an unrealistic degree, you should think of your time spent decluttering as a marathon rather than a sprint which means that slow and steady will win the race every single time.

Finally, if you found this book useful in anyway, a review on is always appreciated!

42924502R00056

Printed in Poland
by Amazon Fulfillment
Poland Sp. z o.o., Wrocław